PROSECCO
PARTY
GAMES

PROSECCO
PARTY
GAMES

ABBIE CAMMIDGE

OVER **25** GAMES

DOG 'n' BONE

Published in 2023 by Dog 'n' Bone Books
An imprint of Ryland Peters & Small Ltd
20–21 Jockey's Fields   341 E 116th St
London WC1R 4BW   New York, NY 10029
www.rylandpeters.com

10 9 8 7 6 5 4 3 2 1

First published in 2018 as *Prosecco Drinking Games*

Text © Abbie Cammidge 2018
Design and illustration © Dog 'n' Bone Books 2018

A CIP catalog record for this book is available from the
Library of Congress and the British Library.

ISBN: 978-1-912983-75-9

Printed in China

Senior designer: Emily Breen
Illustrator: Stephen Dew
Additional illustration: see credits on page 64

CONTENTS

WIN!

LOSE!

BOOZE!

INTRODUCTION

Prosecco is *always* a good idea. There isn't an occasion, celebration, dinner, or night in that can't be enhanced by a sparkling glass of fizz. And while you have a glass in your hand, why not throw a drinking game into the mix to really guarantee a good time, *and* a hangover to match.

Packed full of tips on how to pimp your prosecco and what occasion the game is perfect for, this book will make sure you never have a boring dinner party, quiet night out, or civilized house party ever again. So assemble your girl gang, pour the prosecco, and ladies, get ready to party!

THE GAMES

BEYONCÉ BINGO

PLAYERS: Two or more

YOU'LL NEED: A CD or digital copy of Beyoncé's *Crazy in Love*

PERFECT FOR: Pre-party drinks

PIMP YOUR PROSECCO: A dash of bling-tastic edible 24k gold leaf flakes

All hail queen Bey! Not only has she given us some of the best dancing tunes of the last 20 years, she's about to get you seriously drunk (in love). The rules of this one are pretty simple, but it's VERY effective.

All you need to do is cue up Beyoncé's *Crazy in Love*, pour everyone a LARGE glass of prosecco, and press play. Every time Beyoncé sings the word "crazy," you take a sip. Sounds easy enough, but during the chorus you'll need to sip super-quick and refill if necessary, because the "crazies" come in thick and fast.

If you want to add a competitive element and you're in a large group, then split into two teams—all the single ladies together perhaps? Half of you drink when Bey sings "crazy," the others drink when she sings "love." Extra points for anyone who manages to rock their best Beyoncé moves while playing, without spilling their drink.

FLAMINGLE!

PLAYERS: As many as possible

YOU'LL NEED: A busy bar or dance floor

PERFECT FOR: A wild night out

PIMP YOUR PROSECCO: A flamingo badge, sash, or accessory

The bigger the group, the better for this game. But don't worry if you're short on players, because you can always recruit in the bar—as the name suggests, it's a great one to help you mingle. Be warned, if you and your girls don't like to draw attention to yourselves on a night out it's probably best to turn the page and move on, because this will definitely get you noticed.

To start, you just need to nominate someone in the group to randomly shout "Flamingle!" as loudly as she can. As soon as you hear that word, you have to stop whatever you're doing and stand on one leg like a flamingo and stay balanced in this position for as long as you can. Not easy in high heels! The first person to fall, or put her flamingo leg on the floor has to drain her prosecco. The consolation is she gets to shout "Flamingle" next.

The beauty of this game is you can "Flamingle" all night long, whether it's at the bar, on the dance floor, or even waiting for your takeout pizza at the end of the night.

POP STAR

PLAYERS: Four or more

YOU'LL NEED: Balloons, a pen, and paper

PERFECT FOR: House parties

PIMP YOUR PROSECCO: Add gin and elderflower to make your drink stronger

This is just like a children's birthday party game, except you don't cry when you pop your balloon and, er, you've got a glass of prosecco in your hand and not a lollipop.

To start, you need to write individual dares on small pieces of paper—say two or three dares for each player—and put a different dare inside each balloon. Possible dares could be "let your friend update your social media for the rest of the night," "text a photo of a body part to someone else's boyfriend," or "call your parents and tell them you're pregnant"—you decide how hardcore you want to be.

Blow up the balloons with the dares inside and pour each player a glass of fizz. When you're ready to play, pick one of the balloons at random and place it on a chair. Each player then takes it in turns to sit on the balloon to try and pop it—very tricky with a drink in your hand. Once the balloon pops, the player has to read the dare and make a choice whether to do it or down the prosecco.

GUARANTEED TO GET A PARTY POPPIN' OFF!

CLINK
AND DRINK!

PLAYERS: The more the merrier

YOU'LL NEED: Organized bridesmaids

PERFECT FOR: Bachelorette/hen parties

PIMP YOUR PROSECCO: Gold "Bride Tribe" champagne glass stickers

You know that awkward moment at the beginning of a bachelorette/hen party when people don't really know each other and everyone's making polite chit-chat? Yep? Well this is the game you need to get that ice broken.

A bridesmaid, or the most organized member of the group, needs to write a list of statements before the party, so they're ready to read as soon as the first prosecco bottle is popped open.

The list could include things like "clink and drink if you wish you were a bridesmaid," "clink and drink if you've ever kissed the groom," "clink and drink if you've ever ghosted someone," or "clink and drink if you're wearing matching underwear." The possibilities are endless and the list can be as long as you like.

To play, pour a generous round of prosecco and a bridesmaid will then read out one of the statements from the list. All those who have done the statement in question need to "clink" their glasses with the person next to them and take a good gulp of the drink. After a few rounds, *everyone* will know each other's secrets!

ABOUT LAST NIGHT

PLAYERS: Three or more

YOU'LL NEED: A round of Mimosas and plates of avocado on toast

PERFECT FOR: Weekend brunch

PIMP YOUR PROSECCO: Half fill a glass with prosecco, then top with chilled orange juice and a dash of Triple Sec

The best thing about brunch, other than eggs, is dissecting the group's behavior from the night before. The highs, the lows, the "did she really kiss hims?" It's the perfect time to gossip, over-share, and be each other's therapists. But just because you were drunk last night, doesn't mean the drinking games have to stop.

Go round the group and ask everyone to tell a story—the twist is it could be real or totally made up. The storyteller has to brush up on her acting skills and deliver a performance of a lifetime, while the rest of the group look for signs it's a blatant lie. At the end you have to decide: real or fake. If the storyteller is caught out, she has to down her drink; if she manages to trick the group, then they down theirs.

Play it as many times as you like, and the more outrageous the story the better. Especially if it turns out to be true and you really did sleep with your best friend's brother in the back of her dad's car.

GUESS WHO?

PLAYERS: At least five

YOU'LL NEED: Printouts of body parts

PERFECT FOR: Birthday or bachelorette/hen parties

PIMP YOUR PROSECCO: Add a penis straw—it might be a cliché but it's still a classic

This game requires a bit of prep before hand, so give yourself enough time to get organized. Before the party, email all the guests and ask them to send a picture of a part of their man's body. Chest, abs, knees, shoulders, arms, legs, chin, nose, ears, backside—you can select as many parts as you like depending on how many players you have. Collect all the images and print them out onto pieces of paper.

On the night of the party, get everyone to sit in a circle and pour the prosecco. Everyone other than the bride-to-be or birthday girl is handed a printout, not necessarily the picture they supplied, which they need to conceal until the grand reveal.

Everyone takes it in turns to show their picture and the bride-to-be or birthday girl has to guess what part belongs to whose man. For every wrong answer she has to down her drink, so make sure you have a bottle on standby for top-ups.

If you *really* want to spice things up, throw in a random penis picture and wait to see the reaction it gets, but more importantly who she thinks it belongs to!

THE WALK OF SHAME

PLAYERS: Six or more

YOU'LL NEED: Paper and pens

PERFECT FOR: The morning after the night before

PIMP YOUR PROSECCO: Add equal parts orange juice and prosecco to a glass to make a hangover-friendly Bucks Fizz

Pajamas? Check. Hangover? Check. Shameful story? Perfect. This one's ideal for a lazy Sunday morning after a big party. All you need is some hangover food, a glass of Bucks Fizz to numb the pain, and a whole heap of honesty.

To start, everyone writes down on a piece of paper an embarrassing tale from a previous night out (the kind that involves a lot of alcohol and a loss of dignity), folds it up, and puts it in an empty glass. The group then take it in turns to stand up—if their hangover will allow—pick a story from the glass, and read it out loud. Everyone then has to guess who the story belongs to.

If the group picks the right person first time, the writer of that embarrassing event has to down her drink. The rest of you have to down a drink for every wrong answer you give, until you guess the right person. And if anyone moans about being too hungover to drink, you can tell her it's for her own good. There's nothing like a bit of hair of the dog and a good laugh to get you back on your feet after a big night out.

TIME TO COME CLEAN!

RYAN REYNOLDS

PLAYERS: Three or more

YOU'LL NEED: An encyclopedic knowledge of hot men

PERFECT FOR: Dinner parties with the girls

PIMP YOUR PROSECCO: Add peach purée for a Hollywood classic, the Bellini

There's nothing like a bit of hot-man chat to get a dinner party going. This game will test your knowledge of famous people *and* reveal some weird celebrity crushes.

The game starts off simply enough, but it quickly requires some serious brain power, especially once the pressure's on. Nominate someone at the table to start—all she has to do is say the name of a hot male celebrity. It can be a singer, actor, sports player, or politician; he can be dead or alive, just as long as it's someone she thinks is sexy and it's not the IT guy from work no one's ever heard of.

The person sitting next to the first player then has just five seconds to name another hot male celeb whose name starts with the first letter of the last name of the previous man. So, Tom Hardy could be followed by Harry Styles, followed by Stanley Tucci and so on. The game continues to go around the table in one direction until someone says an alliterative name such as Ryan Reynolds or Matthew McConaughey. The game then changes direction and the person who went previously has to go again.

If anyone fails to think of a man in five seconds, she has to down her drink. The best bit is that under pressure people will claim they think all sorts of random male celebs are good looking, so be sure to challenge their crushes! Simple? Yes. Drunken? Absolutely.

CONSEQUENCES

PLAYERS: At least five

YOU'LL NEED: A pen and paper

PERFECT FOR: Dinner with friends

PIMP YOUR PROSECCO: Add a dash of Chambord raspberry liqueur to your glass

Run out of juicy gossip at dinner with the girls? Time to create your own scandal. However, remember these are just made-up scenarios—don't start spreading any scurrilous rumors, ladies.

Pass a piece of paper and a pen around the dinner table. The first person to play must write a woman's name near the top of the paper, then fold it over so that the name is covered. The next player writes a man's (or woman's) name below, and folds the paper over again to cover the name. The next person writes a location, the next a sexual position, and the final player writes the name of the person who caught them. She then passes the paper to the next person who reads the story out loud to the group.

You can write the name of celebs, real people, fictional characters, or whoever else you can think of. The player who is responsible for the biggest laugh in each round gets to nominate a person to drain her glass of fizz, so be sure to come up with the sort of people and places you think will get a hilarious reaction. You can guarantee that the drunker you get, the more outlandish the scenarios will become.

The rules are: there are no rules!

SHAG, MARRY, CLIFF

PLAYERS: At least two

YOU'LL NEED: Honesty and lots of alcohol

PERFECT FOR: Dinner parties

PIMP YOUR PROSECCO: Make Pornstar Martinis: add vodka and passionfruit Martini mix to a glass and serve with a shot of prosecco

Here's an absolute classic that can be played any time, anywhere, and with any number of people. However, it's definitely best played with a drink in your hand.

If you don't know how to play it already, the rules are super-simple. A player from the group picks three names, perhaps "Bieber, Beckham, and Brad," "Kim, Kourtney, and Khloé," or "Ross, Joey, and Chandler," and asks the person next to them who they would sleep with, who they would marry, and who they would happily throw off the nearest cliff. To add a bit of booze into the mix, apply a strict "drink while you think" rule.

The best thing about drinking while you play this game is the drunker you get the more honest your answers will become. And, remember, you don't have to stick to celebrities, exes, friends' husbands, and bosses should always make an appearance. Be warned though, things can get messy if you start rating people who are in the same room.

NEVER HAVE I EVER

PLAYERS: The more the merrier

YOU'LL NEED: Individual mini bottles of prosecco

PERFECT FOR: Bachelorette/hen weekends

PIMP YOUR PROSECCO: Go all out with mini bottles of Bottega Rose Gold prosecco

Kick off a bachelorette/hen party with this game and everyone will know each other intimately within about half an hour. To play, hand everyone in the group a mini bottle of prosecco and get ready to share.

Take it in turns to go around the group, with the bride-to-be up first. She must say "never have I ever..." followed by a statement such as "sent a naked picture to someone," then everyone who has done that must take a sip of their bottle. Continue around the group, so that each player shares a statement and everyone who has done the thing mentioned in her confession takes a sip of fizz. The first person to finish her bottle is the winner.

Depending on the event and the crowd, you can tailor your statements accordingly. Family games could involve things like "never have I ever peed in the shower" or "never have I ever been pulled over by the police." However, if you're playing at a girls get-together, do feel free to go as X-rated as you dare.

TOPPING UP WITH THE KARDASHIANS

PLAYERS: Two or more

YOU'LL NEED: A TV and an episode of *Keeping up with the Kardashians*

PERFECT FOR: A Friday night in

PIMP YOUR PROSECCO: Drink from a personalized glass

So, like, whether you, like, like the Kardashians or not, they're about to *literally* get the party started. Put on your shortest, tightest outfit, do full hair and makeup, pour a glass of fizz, and get ready, things are about to get "lit."

Between you choose some Kardashian-friendly buzzwords like "literally," "bible," and "doll" and take a sip every time you hear someone on the episode say them. But the fun doesn't end there—every time Kim, Kourtney, Khloé, Kylie, or Kendall takes a selfie you have to down a drink. Let's be honest, if you adopt this rule you're probably going to need a few extra bottles on standby.

The best thing about this game is you can adapt it every time you play. Maybe you drain your drink every time a Kardashian is on her phone or you have to drink every time one of them is in their underwear—your options are endless. Just don't forget to take as many selfies as possible and upload them all to your Instagram!

LIP-SYNC BATTLE

PLAYERS: At least four

YOU'LL NEED: Loads of prosecco, props, and costumes

PERFECT FOR: House parties

PIMP YOUR PROSECCO: Make your own prosecco jello shots

Like karaoke, but better because you don't have to hear everyone's terrible singing voices, this game's perfect for your next house party. Leading up to the party, ask your guests to pick and rehearse miming along to a song of their choice. This way they can practice their dance moves, perfect their facial expressions, and bring any props or costumes they might want to use. For example, if you're going to be Gaga then Coke cans in your hair or a telephone on your head is a must.

At the party each guest must take it in turns to make a grand entrance and lip sync their song. The rest of the group are the judges and each must score them out of five in the following categories: sync-skills, performance, and costume. Keep score of everyone's totals and at the end of the battle award the following: first place wins a bottle of prosecco, second place gets a mini bottle of prosecco, and third place earns a glass of prosecco. The loser must down as many shots as they received points, so in this case, it pays to be *really* terrible. Finally, a glass of prosecco before you perform is a must to help with your performance/make you lose all inhibitions.

14 BAR CRAWL BUBBLES

PLAYERS: At least six

YOU'LL NEED: A pre-made "see and sip" list and lots of bars within close proximity to each other

PERFECT FOR: Birthday nights out

PIMP YOUR PROSECCO: Ask the bar staff to recommend you the best bubbles

If you're planning a night on the town for your birthday, then why not turn every sip into a fun drinking game?

Before you head out, make a list of "see and sip" instructions. It could include things like, "sip when you see a really drunk guy," "sip if the barman flirts with one of the group," "sip if you spot a sketchy fake tan," or "sip if a guy hits on one of the girls." As well as the instructions, you need to create a set of rules for the night too. Things like "down and dance if the DJ plays *About Damn Time*," "take a group selfie in every bar," "do a shot if you get caught texting your boyfriend," or "first person to get ten likes on their Instagram selfie has to do a shot." The options are endless and you can write as many as you like—just save them on someone's phone, share them on your WhatsApp group, or print out a list.

Once you're ready, head to the first bar and make sure everyone in the group has a glass of prosecco, then start the game. Take a sip every time you see something from the list and as soon as the group has finished their drinks move onto the next bar and start again. The speed of drinking and how quickly you drink your prosecco will depend on how long your "see and sip" lists are and how crappy the bar is that you're in!

DIRTY PICTURE

PLAYERS: Four or more

YOU'LL NEED: Pads of paper, pencils, some pre-made "Dirty Pictionary" cards, and a timer

PERFECT FOR: Christmas parties

PIMP YOUR PROSECCO: Two parts prosecco, one part whisky, and a dash of ginger ale—shake, pour, and serve with a side of Christmas cookies

Nothing says Christmas like an evening of over-competitive board-game playing. However, this game is definitely one for you and your friends, *not* your grandma. This is Pictionary, but not as you know it.

Split the group into teams of two. You can either play with a proper Pictionary set and move around the board, use the dice etc, or just give each team a pad of paper and a pen and take it in turns to choose a card and draw. Before you play you have to customize the cards and replace all the words with dirty ones, or create your own set to use.

To play, start by dividing yourselves up into teams of two. One person from a team picks a card and he or she then has one minute to draw an artist's interpretation of what's written down. His or her teammate then has to decipher the scribbles and work out what it says on the card. However, this is "Dirty Pictionary," so forget drawing "a bear with a sore head" or "Big Ben"... Yawn! Mix it up with things like "booty call," "reverse cowgirl," "thong," and "Tinder." It's really up to you how *dirty* you dare take it.

Set the timer and if after one minute the teammate fails to shout out the correct answer, then both players have to down their drinks.

16 GET FRUITY

PLAYERS: As many as possible

YOU'LL NEED: Two oranges and the ingredients to make Aperol Spritz: three parts prosecco, two parts Aperol, and a splash of soda water

PERFECT FOR: Wedding receptions and garden parties

PIMP YOUR PROSECCO: Pop in a slice of orange for the true Italian serve

Aperol Spritz... This old-school Italian aperitif has made a massive comeback in recent years and it's your duty to celebrate it in style by drinking glasses by the bucket load.

Make everyone an Aperol Spritz, get two oranges, split into two teams, and form two lines. The players have to pass the orange down the line, chin to chin, as fast as they can all the way to the end of the line and back again with minimal drink spillage and no hands! The losing team has to down their drinks and make *or* buy the drinks for the winners for the rest of the night.

If you want to turn up the heat, get the boys involved too. Alternate between boys and girls in the line and be prepared to get up close and *very* personal.

DON'T TAKE THE PITH!

RASPBERRY RIPPLE

PLAYERS: Ten or more

YOU'LL NEED: A punnet of raspberries and blueberries

PERFECT FOR: Baby showers

PIMP YOUR PROSECCO: Add raspberry or blueberry bursting bubbles from Popaball

This is a great game to play if no one knows the sex of the mother-to-be's new baby. It also requires you to be super-competitive *and* drink lots of fizz, which is the perfect combo.

Organize the group into two teams—pink or blue depending on if they think the baby is going to be a boy or a girl—but try to keep it as even as possible. Line up a glass of prosecco for each player on a table a couple of meters away and hand each team a punnet of either raspberries or blueberries. Both teams must be armed with the same amount of fruit.

Someone shouts "ready, aim, fire!" and the teams have to throw their fruit into the glasses opposite. The team that gets the most berries in the glasses wins. The losers have to down their drinks, and clean the floor!

18 ICE ICE BABY

PLAYERS: At least six

YOU'LL NEED: Between six and ten ice-cube trays (or more), depending on the size of the group

PERFECT FOR: House parties

PIMP YOUR PROSECCO: Get creative with your choice of straws

The best house parties should always include drunken kitchen dancing, interpretive cocktail-making, and a super-competitive drinking game.

Split the group into two teams and make sure there is one ice-cube tray per team member lined up either side of a table. Fill each one to the top of the cube line with prosecco. Count down from five, then the first person in each line must run to the table and drink each individual ice-cube compartment with a straw, hands held behind their backs. As soon as she has finished her tray, she tags in the next team member. The first team to completely finish all their trays wins.

If you want to make it harder *and* get everyone even more drunk, include two trays per person or top up the trays as the last players are finishing and repeat.

LET'S GET FIZZ-ICAL!

CHERRY BOMB!

PLAYERS: Two or more

YOU'LL NEED: Coupe glasses or champagne saucers, cherries with stems, and a timer (optional)

PERFECT FOR: Picking up guys

PIMP YOUR PROSECCO: Add a few drops of cherry liqueur

Part bobbing for apples, part tongue-twisting challenge, this game feels kind of sophisticated, but actually it's a chance to showcase your naughty side.

Fill old-fashioned, wide-rimmed champagne coupes with prosecco—one glass for each player—and drop a cherry into every glass. Players stand in a line, hands behind their backs, and, after a countdown from three, try to pick up the cherry by the stalk with their teeth.

Once the cherries have been picked the fun really starts. Players then have to try to tie a knot in the cherry stalk with their tongue, which isn't easy especially when everyone's crazy jaw-gymnastics will make it impossible to keep a straight face. The last one to tie the knot has to down her drink. If you like, set a timer for two minutes and everyone who isn't successful before the time is up has to drain her glass.

Now, *apparently* if a girl can tie a cherry stem in a knot with her tongue it means she's an amazing kisser, so this one's ideal with a male audience. Or even better, see if you can recruit some members of the opposite sex for a cheeky boys vs girls challenge.

LOVE ME TINDER

PLAYERS: At least two

YOU'LL NEED: Phones with Tinder accounts

PERFECT FOR: Cocktails with the girls

PIMP YOUR PROSECCO: Ask the bartender to invent you a banging prosecco cocktail

All great love stories start with a match made during a Tinder drinking game, right? OK, so that might not be true, but even though we can't guarantee this game will find you the love of your life, it'll definitely give you a laugh on a night out.

Before you start, make a list of rules and split them into the following categories: "Take a sip," "Halfway," "Down in one," and "Shot." The "Take a sip" category might include things like profile pics of a guy "with his top off," "posed with an animal," or "taking a mirror selfie." If you then swipe and see any of these types of photo on your turn, you take a sip of your drink. You have to down *half* of your drink if you see a "picture with a girl cropped out," a "picture with the boys," or a "gym selfie." You have to down your *whole* drink if you "recognize the guy," "get a crotch shot," or find a "married guy looking for a fling." If you match with the guy *or* come across a man you've already slept with, you have to do a shot.

Once you've established the categories—and you can make up as many as you like—order the drinks and take it in turns to go through your Tinder profiles. Take one swipe then move onto the next player, then the next etc.

SPIN CYCLE

PLAYERS: Four or more

YOU'LL NEED: A large pole/stick/golf umbrella and a garden chair

PERFECT FOR: Summer BBQs and parties

PIMP YOUR PROSECCO: Go cheap and cheerful as a lot of spillage is guaranteed

Get ready ladies, things are about to get messy, very messy. This is perfect for a summer garden party, but make sure you're far away from any pools, open flames, animals, and small children, because you're definitely going to fall over *at least* once.

To set up, push the stick/pole/closed golf umbrella into the grass, then place a garden chair about five yards away. The player up first has to put her head down to the pole and rotate around it five times while holding a bottle of prosecco and an empty glass. The rest of the group can count aloud to help. After the five rotations are completed, the player has to stand up, pour herself a glass, and make her way to the chair as quickly as possible. When she reaches it she has to sit down as elegantly as possible and neck whatever's left in her glass. If the challenge is too easy and there are not enough spills—both liquid and human—add more rotations and move the chair further away.

GUARANTEED TO CAUSE THE SPINS!

PASS THE GLASS

PLAYERS: Eight or more

YOU'LL NEED: Blindfolds and two glasses of prosecco

PERFECT FOR: Pre-party drinks

PIMP YOUR PROSECCO: Make the drinks stronger by adding a shot of vodka or gin

This game might sound simple enough but actually it's pretty tricky, especially because the key to winning is trying not to drink *too* much prosecco, and we all know that's never easy.

Divide the group into teams and form two lines. Everyone is then blindfolded, no peeping, and the person at the start of the line is handed a glass of fizz.

Each person in the line takes a sip and passes the glass down the line, but only the last person can finish the drink. The glass must not be empty before it reaches the end or that team is disqualified. The winners all enjoy a fresh glass of prosecco while the losing team has to take a shot as a forfeit.

Good to the last drop!

BAGS OF FUN

23

PLAYERS: Six or more

YOU'LL NEED: An empty handbag/purse

PERFECT FOR: A plane or train journey with the girls

PIMP YOUR PROSECCO: Go pink with a rosé prosecco

We are all guilty of carrying way too much around in our purses and handbags—old receipts, a hairpin or five hundred, lip gloss, spare underwear, books, you name it. Apparently what you carry in your bag says a lot about you, so why not test your friends and see how well you really know each other.

Everyone in the group secretly takes something out of their bag and places it inside a communal handbag/purse. Take it in turns to select something from the bag and guess who it belongs to. If you guess correctly, the person who the item belongs to downs her drink; if you get it wrong, you down yours. Play it as many times as you like—the more random the items, the better!

LUCKY DIP!

TAKE YOUR PICK!

WHAT'S MY NAME?

PLAYERS: Three or more

YOU'LL NEED: Post-it notes and a permanent marker

PERFECT FOR: Drinks with the girls

PIMP YOUR PROSECCO: Shine bright like a diamond by adding some Popaball rose gold shimmer powder to your glass

We've all played the "Who Am I?" game at some point. This version is, er, the same but better because you have to sing "Ooh na na, what's my name? Ooh na na, what's my name?" to the tune of Rihanna's *What's My Name?* every time a new player starts. So it's even more fun.

The rules of the game are simple. The person who's up first leaves the room while everyone else decides which celebrity she is going to be. Once decided, write the name on a Post-it, call the person back in, and stick it on her forehead so she can't read who she is.

The player then has to work out which celebrity name is on the Post-it by asking questions. Sample questions could be "Am I a man?" "Am I a singer?" "Do I look good naked?" Anything goes as long as the question can be answered with either a "yes"

or a "no." For every "no" the player has to drink, so make sure you have a bottle on standby for top-ups. When she correctly guesses who she is supposed to be, the other players have to drain their glasses. Take it in turns until everyone has had a go at guessing. Rihanna plays this with her girls all the time, honest.

DOWN
A BOTTLE

PLAYERS: Four or more

YOU'LL NEED: Cheap baby bottles

PERFECT FOR: Baby showers

PIMP YOUR PROSECCO: Freeze jelly babies into ice cubes

If you're planning a baby shower and the mama-to-be is a fan of fizz, this is the one to play in her honor. Just because she's not drinking, it doesn't mean her guests have to stick to tea. Play this game in between all the "ooh-ing" and "aw-ing" over booties and blankets and you'll throw a shower to remember.

Hand all the guests a baby bottle, pour a glass of prosecco into each one, and then screw on the teats. The guest of honor gives a countdown from five and then everyone has to drink their bottles as fast as they can. She can also get involved in the game by providing a running commentary, trying to put the rest of you off, and looking out for any cheating, too.

The first person to finish her drink gets to choose someone else from the group who is now only allowed to drink from a baby bottle for the rest of the shower. The last one to finish her drink also has to drink from a bottle until the end of the party.

26 DRUNK JENGA

PLAYERS: Four or more

YOU'LL NEED: Jenga and a permanent marker

PERFECT FOR: Games night

PIMP YOUR PROSECCO: Add a shot of Gordon's pink gin to your glass

If you think Jenga is a great game then prepare to have your mind blown, because this version is the most fun thing ever. Jenga + prosecco + dares = instant games night classic.

Before you start, you need to get creative with your Jenga set and a permanent marker. Take each individual piece and write a dare or instruction on it. For example, on a couple of pieces you could write "down your drink," others could have orders on like "twerk," "remove an item of clothing," or "tell us a secret." You could write "go again," "kiss the person to your right," or "neck the drink to your left." Alternatively, keep it short and simple with things like "Russian," where you have to talk in a Russian accent for the rest of the night, or how about "no eye contact," where you must not look anyone in the eye until the game is over. It's totally up to you.

To play all you need to do is build the Jenga tower so you can't see any of the dares, pour everyone a drink, and take it in turns to slowly select a piece to remove. You then have to do whatever it says on the piece you've chosen. As a final forfeit, whoever knocks down the tower first has to down their drink *and* everyone else's!

THE PROSECCO OLYMPICS

PLAYERS: As many as possible

YOU'LL NEED: Plastic prosecco glasses, plastic picnic cups, tennis balls, sacks/trash bags, rope/string

PERFECT FOR: Summer picnics and garden parties

PIMP YOUR PROSECCO: Add some berries and a scoop of ice cream to your glass to make a prosecco float

Ladies, assemble the teams, tie back your hair, limber up, and (most importantly) pour yourself a drink, because it's time for The Prosecco Olympics. The key to these games being a success is that everyone dresses the part, is ridiculously competitive, and has consumed at *least* two glasses of fizz by the end. Up first is the egg and spoon race, aka Fizzy Balls. The players line up on the starting line, each balancing a tennis ball on top of a glass of prosecco. On the starter's whistle, they have to race to the finish line while balancing their balls and trying not to spill their drink.

Next is the sack race, aka The Splash Race. Everyone lines up in a sack or trash bag, and half fills a plastic picnic cup with prosecco. The players must hold the cups in their teeth as they jump to the finish line. Expect a lot of mess and very sticky faces.

Finally, it's the three-legged race, aka The Drunken Stumble. Pair up with your bestie and tie one of your legs to hers at the ankles. When the whistle's blown, race the other girls to the finish line as fast as you can. Each player must hold a glass of fizz above the head at all times.

The winner of each game gets to nominate a person to do a prosecco-based forfeit, which the contestant in last place will also have to do.

28 PIMP MY PROSECCO

PLAYERS: Four or more

YOU'LL NEED: A variety of mixers, spirits, drink accessories, a pack of cards, and some prosecco

PERFECT FOR: House parties

PIMP YOUR PROSECCO: Keep your eyes peeled for cool, vintage glasses

This is cocktail-making with a twist. The twist being you don't know if you're going to invent the next Singapore Sling or make your friend throw up. Fun!

Set up a bar with a wide variety of mixers, spirits, glasses, accessories, and, of course, prosecco. Think different fruits, prosecco shimmer powder, cocktail umbrellas, straws... Anything you can think of. Lay out a pack of cards on the bar and each player must take it in turns to select a card from the pack. The first person to get a queen selects a spirit and adds a shot to a glass. The next player to get a queen chooses a mixer and adds it to the glass, the next person who picks a queen chooses the accessory.

Whoever finds the final queen has to top the glass with prosecco and drink the "cocktail." Fingers crossed it's a good one! Once all the queens are gone, reshuffle the deck and get ready to play again.

SPIN THE BOTTLE

PLAYERS: Five or more, boys and girls

YOU'LL NEED: Spirits, shot glasses, an empty bottle of prosecco, and a few full ones

PERFECT FOR: Pre-gaming for a big night out

PIMP YOUR PROSECCO: Up the ante with some Patrón Tequila Coffee Liqueur

The last time you played this game you probably had braces, questionable dress sense, were drinking warm alcopops, and were praying the bottle pointed to your crush. This version is much the same, but the drinks have improved and hopefully your fashion choices have too.

Assemble the group into a circle and place an empty bottle of prosecco in the middle. In front of each player place a glass of prosecco *and* a shot or your chosen spirit.

Take it in turns to spin the bottle. Whoever the bottle points to, the person spinning gets to decide: he or she can either drink the prosecco, do the shot, *or* kiss the person the bottle's pointing to. After a few spins and downed drinks the options will start to reduce, then you'll have to get ready to pucker up.

ACKNOWLEDGMENTS

A massive thanks to all my girls who definitely put the *pro* in prosecco.
Especially Rosie, Liv, Jane, Carrie, Amy, Ruth, Sarah, Rachael, Nadia, and Ron.
And my best boys Jodie, Buddy, Spike, and Manny.

PICTURE CREDITS

Front cover Jacquie Boyd/Getty Images. Page **3** right VasjaKoman/Getty Images; **8** and **9** helen_tosh/Getty Images; **10** Dmitry Volkov/Getty Images; **11** VasjaKoman/Getty Images; **12** beemore/Getty Images; **14** and **15** VasjaKoman/Getty Images; **16** drante/Getty Images; **19** main image SaulHerrera/Getty Images; **19** insert image vectorikart/Getty Images; **20** VasjaKoman/Getty Images; **23** Joseph McDermott/Getty Images; **24** SaulHerrera/Getty Images; **27** VasjaKoman/Getty Images; **28** SaulHerrera/Getty Images; **31** Jacquie Boyd/Getty Images; **32** SaulHerrera/Getty Images; **35** studiostoks/Shutterstock; **36** Jacquie Boyd/Getty Images.
All other illustrations by Stephen Dew.